KATHRYN M. IRELAND

TIMELESS INTERIORS

KATHRYN M. IRELAND

TIMELESS INTERIORS

PHOTOGRAPHS BY TIM BEDDOW

GIBBS SMITH
TO ENRICH AND INSPIRE HUMANKIND

To Victoria,
A client, a friend, and an inspiration. A tireless
partisan on behalf of her family, her work, and her
philanthropy—and all who are dear to her heart.

First Edition
16 15 14 13 12   5 4 3 2

Text © 2012 Kathryn M. Ireland
Photographs © 2012 Tim Beddow except as noted below:
Pages 152,153,156,158,159,163,164,165 © 2012 Andreas von Einsiedel

Published by
Gibbs Smith
P.O. Box 667
Layton, Utah 84041
1.800.835.4993 orders
www.gibbs-smith.com

Designed by Rita Sowins / Sowins Design
Printed and bound in China

Gibbs Smith books are printed on either recycled, 100% post-consumer waste,
FSC-certified papers or on paper produced from sustainable PEFC-certified
forest/controlled wood source. Learn more at www.pefc.org.

Library of Congress Cataloging-in-Publication Data

Ireland, Kathryn M.
  Kathryn M. Ireland timeless interiors / Kathryn M. Ireland ; photographs by
Tim Beddow. — First Edition.
    pages cm
  ISBN 978-1-4236-3031-9
1. Ireland, Kathryn M.—Themes, motives. 2. Interior decoration—Themes,
motives. I. Beddow, Tim. II. Title.
  NK2004.3.I73A4 2012
  747—dc23
                    2012017368

CONTENTS

FOREWORD

There is nothing more comforting and sexy than intimate spaces. When these two feelings come together in one room, the result feels magical. Anyone who has ever visited Kathryn's Santa Monica home has experienced this firsthand. She is a master at setting the mood.

Having met hundreds of designers in my career, I can tell you there is no one quite like Kathryn Ireland, and I am quite sure everyone in the design industry would agree. She has a vivre for life that makes you want to drop everything and run away with the circus. I always find myself feeling swept away when I spend an hour with her and can only imagine how anyone feels if they are lucky enough to have a home filled with her high energy and appreciation for the past.

It's a wonder to me how she can use so many different patterns and textures, surround them with found objects and antiques and make them all feel woven together with ease.

I hope you will enjoy getting swept away, as I have, when reading through the pages of Kathryn's latest book.

—Michael Bruno
Founder, 1stdibs

INTRODUCTION

As with any exciting romance, the secret to mutual giddiness and gratification is inexplicable chemistry. An interior decorator can have a client with exquisite taste, a bottomless budget, endless time, outrageous sophistication, and totally motivated to work well together; but if there's no synergy, it's a non-starter, because good vibrations can't be fabricated. The unpredictable spark with a client that inspires gorgeous work may be fickle, but it's the source for what, in my experience, is the sine qua non of a knock-out residence.

I always say the client makes the decorator. That's what this book is about. Of the eight homes I selected for my fourth book, the common denominator is the extraordinary rapport that developed between the client and me. And it shows. These photographs represent every variation of constructive and creative interaction. Sometimes the client wants to be completely hands-on, sometimes less so. Sometimes it's love at first sight, and sometimes the love evolves. But in every case, the joy of spirited collaboration is embedded in the work and still reflects back to me over time. I am always blindsided when this magic happens. Despite some push me/pull you moments, working on these homes with each and every client was a joy in real time and a joy in retrospect.

And it was fun. That's why I keep doing it.

A
SPANISH
REVIVAL
HOME

When I moved to Los Angeles, the architecture that really turned my head was Spanish Colonial Revival. With a distinctive vocabulary of thick adobe walls, recessed windows, decorative wrought-iron work, and terra-cotta-tiled roofs, the style became emblematic of the California look and is perfect for a benign, balmy climate that allows indoor/outdoor living all year long. When I bought my first house, I bought in this style, and renovating it taught me what works and what's absurd in the Spanish Colonial Revivals built between the World Wars of the last century, the heyday of the design. A few years ago I completed a full-scale restoration of a ravishing Wallace Neff design in Ojai, California, one of the highlights of my career. So when my client Leslie Burke acquired a 1924 Roland E. Coate house in Palos Verdes, I was thrilled to work on another Spanish Colonial Revival by a marquee architect. On my first visit, I was bowled over by the spectacular views of Catalina Island and Santa Monica Bay from the terrace. Worth

every moment braving the elements in the dead of a Southern California winter—cardigan weather!

From the exterior, the rambling house exudes classic Spanish Colonial Revival charm, complete with a canopy of bougainvillea tumbling over the entrance. Upon entering, I was anxious to see the spatial orientation of the rooms, the condition of the woods, plastered walls and tiles. I was curious to discover what was left of the Coate original. I couldn't have been more delighted. The house was in pristine condition. With whitewashed plaster walls, minimal window treatments, and typical high ceilings, a well-preserved Spanish Colonial Revival is a canvas. Once you're inside, almost anything works. Almost.

Leslie and I edited the furnishings from her contemporary former home down to a handful of items—including a grand piano—and I went to work, bearing in mind that the house would be inhabited by four children, so comfort and resiliency were key. We shopped locally in L.A. at my favorite haunts for authentic furnishings and accessories that would underscore the tradition of the style but not dominate the overall look.

The Murano glass fixture over the kitchen table, bedroom chairs, and a contemporary Tim Woolcock painting were found on a European buying

Right and above:
Sofa and chair fabrics from
Rogers & Goffigon. Lamps
and shades from Rooms
and Gardens, Santa Monica.
Vintage textile pillows from
KMI Studio, West Hollywood.
Antique wooden candlesticks
from Dos Gallos, Los Angeles.

trip. After mentioning to Robert Kime on a walk in the English countryside that I was on the lookout for a really magnificent four-poster bed for my client's master bedroom, he led me to one of his barns. Inside, he showed me a rare nineteenth-century Anglo-Indian bed with a fabulous checkered history that included a tour of duty at a palace in Jaipur! This showstopper is now the centerpiece of the most regal room in the house.

The living room is formally arranged, but I conceived the parlor beyond it as a relaxed family room. In both spaces, the comfort factor is palpable. The doors and windows embrace the vistas as part of the room's décor. I kept the color palette neutral—in washed whites, rich creams, and soft caramels—to temper the dark wood of exposed beams and flooring.

Accent pillows, lamp shades and rugs provide kicks of color and pattern and enliven the light-drenched spaces. Once the interiors were complete, I brought in Stephen Block from Inner Gardens to landscape the grounds and gardens. Stephen accented informal terraces with potted Mediterranean stalwarts that flourish in hot, dry climates by the coast—lavender, geranium, and rosemary—and orchestrated the grounds with native plantings, creating an authentic sense of place for the timeless design that Roland E. Coate initiated ninety years ago.

Above and facing:
The butcher's block, which we found on 1stdibs
from Antiques on Old Plank Road, Chicago, serves
as a workstation and dish pantry. Cushion fabrics on
custom wooden banquette from Claremont, C&C
Milano and Colefax and Fowler. My "go-to" wicker
Lloyd Loom chairs are practical, comfortable, and
have great style. Venetian bell light fixture from
Blanchard Antiques, London. Roman shades and
the KMI Studio walnut Shaker-style table keep the
breakfast nook uncluttered, simple, and easy.

"Art has always been important in my homes, mixing landscapes, portraits and abstracts. I like to find the unexpected every so often in a room." —LESLIE BURKE

Facing:
Painting by Tim Woolcock, from Mark Ransom, London. Antique Spanish chess table from Hacienda, Ojai, California. Mexican dripware from KMI, West Hollywood.

Facing:
Custom-made walnut trestle table from Country Gear, Bridgehampton, New York. KMI Studio Italian dining chairs upholstered in Robert Kime "Indian Pear" and Rogers and Goffigon "Cyclades." Oil painting by Sherrie McGraw over Italian 18th-century chest. Sconces, circa 1920s, with Vaughan shades. Amadi Carpets rug.

Above:
A Lalique vase holds flowers from the garden. Bernardaud china with antique French glassware. Flatware by Christofle. Moroccan votive holders.

French daybed in the dressing room from Rosemary McCaffrey Antiques, Santa Monica, upholstered in Chelsea Textiles "Tan Wisteria." Antique fabric pillows from Mary Jane McCarty. Inlaid side table from Dan Marty Design. Amadi Carpets rug. Dressing table from Valerie Wade, London. Dressing table chair from KMI Studio, West Hollywood. Murano chandelier client's own.

A BEVERLY HILLS COTTAGE

Many of my clients and I start off as my friends and, luckily, end as friends! Such was the case with Joe and Debbie Mannis. As a couple, they share a passion for fine art photography, the work of West Coast pop and contemporary artists, and confidence in their aesthetic instincts. Debbie is also an enthusiastic collector of Native American folk art, relics, and religious artifacts. My marching orders were to pull it all together—their art, antiques, and flea market finds with new upholstered pieces, window treatments, and accessories—into harmonious, "un-decorated" interiors for the couple's new address in Beverly Hills. Because my friends are aesthetic heavyweights, there was no hand-holding. Joe and Debbie just needed a fresh set of eyes to sequence things and recognize opportunities they were missing due to familiarity. We started with their incredible collection of art and went from there …

Here in the living room, we left the exposed brick fireplace naturally distressed. It's nothing special, but with three Ed Ruscha prints from the Gasoline Stations series, the wall space above becomes the focal point of the room.

"We were adamant that the house be unpretentious and under-decorated and that it showcase pieces from our travels that we love—what Kathryn does best. The artwork was the focus for us, but comfort was key." —JOSEPH MANNIS

Facing:
The photograph by Philip-Lorca diCorcia occupies a prominent spot in the living room. A large 19th-century Papago Indian pot sits atop a vintage wicker sideboard that Debbie found for "next to nothing." Through a sliver of doorway, Ed Ruscha's *The End #24* can be seen on the entryway wall.

Above:
Looking from the entryway
into the living room,
the shaggy fantastical
animal standing next
to a KMI Studio Wilbury
armchair is a stunning
piece of Navajo folk art.

Facing:
A simple French provincial table in the
entryway displays Spanish *santos* figures
and a Plains Indian possible bag from
the 1880s. Three drawings are Ed Ruscha:
top left, the spine of the Steinbeck
book *Of Mice and Men*; top right and
bottom from the *Shattered Glass* series.

Before I came on board, Debbie had chosen the Benjamin Moore Driftwood Grey wall color as a backdrop for Ruscha *Gasoline Stations* photographs. I grew to love the neutral bisque-like tone, which has a curiously enveloping quality that creates an intimate cocoon for dining. The vibrant embroidered Indian cloth of burnt orange, golden saffron, and rich crimson on the dining table warms things up and gives the room all the color it needs. While sifting through Debbie's remarkable collection of pottery, these Picasso Madoura ceramic owls jumped out at me. Their naïf quality works effortlessly with the rustic handcrafting of the cloth. On the sideboard, a large vintage Bauer vase in very rare red brown enhances the earthy vibe of the room. And Ruscha and Picasso hold up their end of the conversation.

Left:

We anchored Joe's den with a custom-made nine-foot sofa with added depth for extra seating, extra comfort, and impromptu napping. The existing pair of Ralph Lauren leather club chairs flank the Chinese coffee table from Lief, West Hollywood. Ed Ruscha's 1982 *One Night Stand Forever* is the undisputed star of the room; Debbie's pottery collection meanders throughout, adding visual interest to the built-in bookshelves. Early 20th-century Acoma Pueblo pottery and Cochiti Pueblo animals mix it up with art books and a ceramic peach by artist Mineo Mizuno. Striped pillows, inspired by Navajo trade blankets, stay true to room's New Mexico subplot.

Facing:

A colorful Mexican serape, red paisley window treatments, leather chairs and contemporary sculpture make the old-fashioned eat-in kitchen multi-culti and festive. The Liza Lou beaded Comet can from her *Kitchen* installation is displayed on a stand custom made for the piece.

Above:

In renovation-happy Los Angeles, finding this pristine period kitchen was a stroke of incredible good fortune. Debbie didn't have to do anything except for press her collection of vintage Bauer into everyday service and stack it on open shelving where it looks terrific. An old Mexican trough at the end of the room provides storage for the outdoor pillows in bad weather.

For twenty years the Mannises lived in a mid-century modern house in Bel Air. Their home was an archetypal expression of California modernism with its post and beam, sliding glass door, and open floor plan design. But eventually, they wanted a house that had the convenience of a condo, without much upkeep, and easy access to restaurants, book stores, and shopping. So they moved east to Beverly Hills, above the storied Sunset Strip. With its rose-draped exterior, their new picturesque house resembles a cottage transplanted from England's Lake District. Set on a hilltop with four great exposures, at any given time of day one of the rooms is bathed in California sunshine.

The bedroom for a couple can become a contest between masculine and feminine, old and edgy, or minimal and chintzy. Here in the master there was no need for a diplomatic compromise. We all agreed on soft hues of yellow and tan in subtle prints. In a room filled with natural light, even the brightest yellow will read paler. The net effect is a comfortable and calm refuge for both Mannises. We repurposed a pair of formal Chinese lamps by removing the wood bases and making new lamp shades. A paisley print from my first collection upholsters a hand-carved headboard from KMI Studio.

A
FILM
DIRECTOR'S
HOME

Film director Robert Zemeckis—Bob, to his friends—bought the house next door to his bachelor residence in Montecito with the idea of building a contemporary barn to use as a creative work space and screening facility; he hired acclaimed Santa Barbara–based architect Andy Neumann to design the structure. But life changed for Bob when he became engaged to his beautiful wife, Leslie, during the architectural process. With a family in mind, Andy had to go back to the drafting table and turn the screening room into a home. Fortunately, making radical mid-course corrections comes with the territory for directors, architects, and interior decorators. So when Bob wanted a stylish great room that could become a screening room at the push of a button, then that's what I would do. I merely had to camouflage the projection port with a large painting that could rise mechanically for screenings.

Previous overleaf:
Dining table from Hollyhock,
Los Angeles. Custom-made
George III–style chairs by
Burton-Ching, San Francisco.
Painting by R. Kenton Nelson,
Pasadena. Glass sconces from
Karl Kemp Antiques, New York.

Right:
The mix of more traditional
furniture with Neumann's
clean, contemporary
architecture achieved an
overall effect of comfort
and function, as well as
being a place to gather.
Sofa fabric Cowtan & Tout
"Stanton Weave." Chair
fabric Glant "Lombardia
Stripe." Carpets from J.H.
Minassian & Co, Los Angeles.

When I found a large gold 18th-century Italian Baroque fretwork panel in London, I immediately visualized it as a headboard for Bob and Leslie's Venetian flight of fancy. Luxurious red damask fabric from Nina Campbell's "Loire Silk" collection upholsters the walls, imparting a depth of color not attainable with paint or wallpaper. Bedcover fabric from Coraggio Textiles.

Above and facing:

The master bedroom is inspired by the couple's lavish honeymoon suite in Venice; Bob and Leslie wanted to capture the dark, mysterious, romantic allure of that Italian city—a shock, I think, to the architect, whose contemporary structure was now going to concede territory to a room boldly reminiscent of doge-era Venice. But Andy was very gracious and understanding. An upholstered KMI Wilbury armchair and ottoman framed by grand curtains creates a great reading and lounging space in the master bedroom. Using the red damask wall fabric for the curtains sustains the opulent mood and evokes a bygone era. Standing lamp from Christopher Hodsoll, London. Needlepoint pillows from Vaughan.

"When we started the project, Bob was a bachelor. The main living area was seen as a large barn-like art studio space and screening room. However, it had to be able to be used as a more conventional living-dining room in the future, "just in case." The barn fit well into the rural context and the white board and batt exterior tied in nicely with the house next door, only crisper." —ANDY NEUMANN

Since Leslie is a baker, she necessarily had a lot of input into the design of the kitchen. The flooring was the inspiration for the color palette, so we went with colors of the harvest—wheat, flax, and cream—staples of any *boulangerie*. Light fixture over pine table from Country Gear, Bridgehampton, NY. Lighting over the island from Historical Materialism, NYC. Kathryn M. Ireland sheer on windows.

The den is the primary gathering space for the Zemeckis family, which now includes three children. Although Bob's ex-bachelor house next door has been turned into office suites, guest quarters, and a large playroom, this living area off the kitchen is where everyone naturally congregates. Divided from the kitchen by a pony wall, the family room opens onto a large terrace with outdoor kitchen facilities and pizza oven. The custom-made deep, oversized tufted leather sofa by KMI Studio was inspired by an old English leather Chesterfield. The ottoman is upholstered in a de Le Cuona paisley. Tables and table lamps from Blanchard Antiques, London. Gardens designed by Nancy London.

A SANTA BARBARA HORSE RANCH

While I was renovating the Libbey Ranch in Ojai, I got a call from a dynamic, well-traveled couple that had just bought a 400-acre ranch near Santa Barbara that needed decorating. The wife described it as a top to bottom job and invited me to come and see the property as soon as possible. I thought before visiting her ranch that maybe she should visit mine. She remarked that unlike the Wallace Neff estate I was working on, her house was all about the view and landscape, not the architecture. The main residence of the appropriately named Hilltop was a nondescript, early 1990s horseshoe-shaped house at the summit of the property. But what a property! It's pure view everywhere you look—boundless sky, the Pacific Ocean that goes on forever, and the majestic Santa Barbara mountain range. For clients who need a peaceful retreat as a home base, the landscape of rolling hills would calm the nerves of the most jangled workaholic. It did mine.

Above:
The clients' chairs were re-covered in yellow leather from Ashbury Hides, Los Angeles. Antique Mexican tile inserts colorfully accent the fireplace. Drawing by Diego Rivera. Eighteenth- and 19th-century artifacts complete this intimate vignette.

Right:
Even an overlooked corner can be turned into a cozy sitting area. The L-shaped bench by KMI Studio is covered in Claremont "Toile de Tours." Table from Michael Haskell, Montecito, CA.

But the house itself was a problem. Though it had great and abundant space, the bad flow pattern over-complicated the interiors. The clients' marching orders were a decorator's dream. Do what you want.

When I asked the lady of the house to describe how she wanted the place to feel, she replied, "Somewhere exotic, like Mexico or Morocco." Enamored of indigenous Latin American architecture of earthy materials, my client's taste also extended to Moroccan style. She wanted to draw on the inspiration of these colorful cultures for her California home. In that spirit, I segued into a fearless mode of vibrant colors and bold motifs. There was just one condition: the entire compound—main residence, outdoor terraces and gardens, plus a handful of guest cottages—had to be completed by Thanksgiving, just three months away. There was no time to panic. I started immediately. But as we got into the work, my clients and I realized the importance of new tile for the bathrooms and kitchens. Not usually a problem, unless your client wants custom-made, handcrafted, artisanal tile from Fez!

Facing:
The clients' dining table from a previous residence fit perfectly here. Fabrics from Robert Kime and wall coloring by Olivia Raeburn help re-create the ambience of Old Mexico. Rustic chandelier and antique hand-carved cupboard found on 1stdibs.

Facing:

A chandelier is the head-turner in any room, even the kitchen. I dressed this one down with fabric-covered lamp shades in a variety of whimsical prints for the candles. Character was added by re-facing the cupboards with cut-out star designs and covering the stovetop backsplash and adjacent walls with Moroccan tiles. The butcher's block, found at Dienst and Dotter in Sag Harbor (now in NYC), is one of my favorite pieces.

Above:

A painting by Laura Fiume from R.E. Steele Antiques, East Hampton, NY, animates the wall space over the fireplace. I sourced the mantel's reclaimed timber from a Northern California salvage house. The inlaid tiles of the fireplace surround from Exquisite Surfaces, Beverly Hills, keep the Moroccan theme going in the sitting room.

Above:
African bead chair with
a cushion made from an
antique Pakistani ralli from
Josh Graham, London,
next to an Indian pouf.

Facing:
Layering of pattern and texture
resulted in a family room that's
fanciful and fun. Lloyd Loom chairs
by Loom Italia are staples in all of
my kitchens. Chandelier and table
from Lucca, West Hollywood.

"Since California has been Kathryn's stomping ground for many years, she's learned a relaxed European sensibility with the hot hues appropriate to the sun-drenched coastline. At Hilltop, she has mingled Mexican and Moroccan styles, using reds and pinks that vie with the bougainvillea." —TIM BEDDOW, PHOTOGRAPHER

Facing:
I saw these vintage serapes in Hacienda, Ojai, CA, and wanted the exuberant color and vivid patterns for the hallway. Kathryn M. Ireland red ribbed fabric made them floor length. Light fixtures from Blanchard Antiques, London. Hallway chairs from Michael Haskell, Montecito. Floor runners from Amadi Carpets, West Hollywood.

Above:
Nineteenth-century Indian embroidered
bedcover from Michael Haskell, Montecito, and
embroidered pillow from KMI, West Hollywood.
Area rug from Amadi Carpets. Desk and chair by
Jacques Adnet. Lamps from Pat McGann Gallery.

Facing:
Anglo-Indian carved chairs from Christy's A & D
Warehouse, Sag Harbor, NY. A Moroccan water
seller's bag from KMI, West Hollywood, and inlaid
Syrian mirror sourced on 1stdibs ornament the
wall. Curtain and sofa fabrics by Raoul Textiles.

With only three months to design and furnish the interiors, restructuring work was confined to opening up the dark entry hall. Though risky considering the time restraint, I felt it was imperative. Elsewhere, floors were taken up and replaced and false ceilings were taken down. But the most legible alteration to the house was the addition of custom tiles from Morocco on walls and floors. Miraculously, they were handcrafted, shipped, and installed within the twelve-week time frame. My client insisted that they were integral to imbuing the space with a sense of authenticity. And she was right.

The plantation shutters on the bathroom windows were among the few design elements from the original house that we decided to retain. The Berber rug was found on a buying trip to Marrakesh.

Facing:
For the daughter's bedroom, a cacophony of pinks and florals. The Portuguese bed was found in pieces, and then reconstructed, at Woodwright Furniture in Santa Barbara. A chair from Ruby Beets in Sag Harbor is upholstered in an antique Pakistani ralli. The room is a collision of colorful fabrics from Pierre Frey, Raoul Textiles, and John Robshaw.

Above:
The tiles lining the open shower and bathroom walls were ordered from Mosaic House, NYC. Graphic multi-pink rug from Pat McGann Gallery. Vintage Mexican folk art chair found at the Rose Bowl flea market, Pasadena.

Right:
Gardens and grounds should
also be an expression of a
home's personality. Oversized
Guatemalan hammocks
from Dos Gallos Antique
Furniture in L.A. drape
across terraces all over the
property. Informal terraces
flourish with native plants.

Blankets of fuchsia
bougainvillea were growing
around and about the terraces.
My greatest challenge was
to impart a sense of age to
the ranch house and make
it look as if it was from the
1890s instead of the 1990s.
The established bougainvillea
was a perfect accomplice!

The horse barn, built in the early 1990s, was meticulously planned and executed. The stable overlooks riding rings, a polo field, and the Pacific Ocean—and the horses have the best view on the property.

THE HORSE RANCH COTTAGES

When it came time to decorate the one- and two-bedroom cottages spread out across the rolling hills, I was fortunate to be working with celebrated architect and old friend Marc Appleton. He had built the guest cottages on the footprints left by a handful of mobile homes. Together we set out to re-create the magic of our first collaboration—model rooms at San Ysidro Ranch, the iconic California resort hotel. Thematically, Marc and I designed the cottages to relate to the main residence and to maintain the unpretentious, laid-back tradition of ranch living. I sourced unique furnishings and artifacts from three continents to create cozy environments with just enough quirk to keep them interesting and a dash unexpected. There isn't one item I bought just to fill a spot. Everything—from the largest painting to the smallest demitasse cup—has a story. When the cottages were complete, the entire ranch compound really felt like a world within a world. What had begun as my clients' dream finally ended as one.

A couple of 19th-century bergéres are reupholstered in Pakistani rallis and Kathryn M. Ireland "Casablanca" fabric. The card table and chairs, purchased in Southwest France, were reupholstered in Kathryn M. Ireland "George" woven fabric. Coffee table from R.E. Steele, East Hampton; Catalina tile side table is a local find. Curtains are Kathryn M. Ireland "Safi Suzani Fiesta."

Above:
Work table from Robert
Stilin, East Hampton, NY.
Artwork by New York
City street artists. In each
cottage kitchen, the
cabinets are painted bright,
coordinating colors.

Facing:
The clients' existing table
and chairs shine under a light
fixture from Henry Beguelin.
Curtain fabric is Kathryn M.
Ireland "Safi Suzani." Custom
lamp shade enhances a lamp
found in Santa Barbara.

The cottage overlooking the polo field comes with fireplaces in the living room and master bedroom. Paintings over the mantel are from Laurin Copen Antiques, Bridgehampton, NY. Painting on wall from Paris flea market at Clignancourt. Bird paintings on desk by Los Angeles artist Baby De Selliers. Candlesticks from Obsolete, Venice, CA. Bed from Michael Smith.

Facing:
A Vaughan lamp sits on an antique Mexican desk from KMI, West Hollywood. Chair upholstered in red and white stripe from Indigo Seas, Los Angeles. Silver mirror from Hacienda, Ojai.

Above:
The Waterworks bathroom fittings and fixtures contribute to the vintage ambience of the cottage style. Mirrors from Big Daddy Antiques, Culver City, CA. All accessories from KMI, West Hollywood.

Hedge Cottage might be the smallest of the
cottages, but it's the only one with two bedrooms.
Roger Capron coffee table from Blackman Cruz, L.A.
Leather and nail side tables and Indian twisted wood
candlestick lamps from KMI, West Hollywood.

Facing:
Mexican leather table
and chairs from California
Auctioneers, Ojai. Fabric
from KMI "Mexico Meets
Morocco" collection. Light
fixture from Henry Beguelin.

Above:
Atop a vintage Mexican side table,
a lamp fashioned from a massive
French wine bottle clad in woven
twigs. Throw pillow made from
Pakistani ralli fabric. South African
tent poles adorn the mantel.

Above:
I found this geometric wall art at Urban Country, Venice, CA. Originally purchased for the communal "pub" recreation cottage, the painting was orphaned until I realized the cottages' laundry room would be the perfect home for this vibrant statement piece. All you need for any small space is something succinct and bold.

Facing:
Everyone knows I'm not shy about using color, but it was my client's idea to paint the cabinets bright yellow, the perfect pop to balance out the soft white walls and neutral flooring. Center island from Ruby Beets Sag Harbor, NY. Inlaid wagon train tile bought at auction. Custom handcrafted doors from Woodwright Furniture, Santa Barbara. Knobs from McKinney & Co., London.

Overhead lighting from Obsolete, Venice, CA. The pair of mirrors over pedestal sinks began their careers at a funfair! Carpet from Amadi Carpets, West Hollywood. Mexican *retablo* painting in ornate gilt frame from Michael Haskell, Montecito. Wall sconces by Vaughan Lighting.

Left:
Marc Appleton used recycled woods in the construction of this building. The Dutch door opens out onto a dining terrace, the sine qua non of California living. Laura Fiume artwork hangs on the far wall.

Above:
A vintage '60s hanging leather football chair from Blackman Cruz articulates the far corner. Geometric artwork flanking the wall-mounted TV from Urban Country, Venice. Vintage 1950s foosball table from Eccola, Los Angeles.

This recreation room was inspired by the lounge at the San Ysidro Ranch. Marc Appleton used reclaimed timber in sizes almost impossible to acquire these days. The textural quality of the wood endows the room with a rugged counterpoint to the pop colors and furnishings. The 19th-century haberdasher's table from Adesso Imports, Los Angeles, was repurposed as the bar top. Wall sconces by Troy Lighting. Bar stools from Henry Beguelin.

"The cottages looked like they would be a fun exercise in creating a recreational compound that would be a charming and peaceful retreat for our client's frequent ranch guests—and Kathryn, Art Luna and I did indeed have fun putting it together!" —MARC APPLETON

The client wanted this cottage to be more tranquil than the others. I started with comfortable furniture and finished with muted prints and tones of stone, straw, and lettuce green, colors that are very soothing to me. Abstract painting by Tim Woolcock. Pair of horseshoe stools from JF Chen, Los Angeles. Coffee table from Obsolete, Venice. Pair of green lamps from Laurin Copen Antiques, Bridgehampton, NY. All fabrics by Kathryn M. Ireland.

Left:
The antique French oval pine
table from Robert Stilin, East
Hampton, NY, is surrounded by
Lloyd Loom chairs by Loom Italia.
Chandelier from Lucca Antiques,
West Hollywood. Curtain fabric is
Kathryn M. Ireland "Paisley Stripe."

Above:
A rustic 18th-century French
stool serves as an end table to
a Mission-style chair from the
1920s. Back cushion fashioned
from a Moroccan tribal rug.

The patchwork quilt is made with fabrics from my first collection in a pale juniper blue-green customized to coordinate with the "Moroccan Stripe" curtain fabric. Walls upholstered in KMI "Toile Silvertree." The overall effect is a bedroom with a soft and restful mood. Boudoir lamps from Ruby Beets.

A PLAYWRIGHT'S HOME

When David Mamet and Rebecca Pigeon relocated to the West Coast from Boston some years ago and camped out at my house in Santa Monica, they fell in love with the area and decided to find a home close by. Their requirements were modest: they wanted a livable family home with a good floor plan and a gracious flow from room to room to room. And that's what they got. The Mamets came across a house designed in the 1930s by John Byers, an architect renowned for his Spanish Colonial Revival and Monterey-style residences. What I love about the Southern California houses built between the First and Second World Wars is that the architects of that period, Byers among them, understood that exterior living spaces were as important as the interiors. So they created lovely interior fluidity through clear, distinct rooms and plenty of garden and patio space for outdoor living. Walking into the Mamets' always has that feeling of a comfortable home particularly attuned to Southern California.

The study off the living room has French doors that lead
out to the patio and garden. The fireplace with Malibu
tile surround is original to the house. Window treatments
are Kathryn M. Ireland Woven "Brianza Jacquard."

Above:
A built-in bookcase in
the living room shows off
some of David's movie
memorabilia and his prized
collection of first editions.

Left:
An antique English pine
cupboard houses a collection
of vintage Bauer pottery.
Alabaster light fixture from
Lief, West Hollywood.

Right:
Modernizing the kitchen and
bathrooms required some
reshuffling of the floor plan.
The old kitchen was cramped
and had neither a view nor
access to the lush greenery of
the backyard. So we turned
it into a laundry room/mud
room with a good work
station for Rebecca and built
this kitchen on the site of the
former dining room. With large
windows overlooking the pool
and French doors that open
out onto the courtyard, the
kitchen now feels spacious,
secluded and surrounded
by nature. Diamond-painted
floor by Olivia Raeburn.

Facing:
Queenie, the family's marvelous Labradoodle, has a bed in every room. Here in the kitchen area, she lounges on leather cushions from Ashbury Hides. Although the built-in Mission-style finished carpentry looks as though it was original to the house, we actually had it all designed and custom-crafted by Woodwright Furniture in Santa Barbara.

Above:
The cloth on the kitchen table is an antique English patchwork quilt. Classic Windsor chairs from Christopher Howe, London, available through KMI online. Parchment shades are an easy, unobtrusive window treatment that translates an occasionally harsh California sunlight into a warm glow.

With generous vaulted ceilings and dormer windows, the master bedroom feels like a converted English attic but, in fact, it's located on the first floor. David added a piece of his own design—the bed! The fabrics from de Le Cuona, Robert Kime, and Kathryn M. Ireland collaborate beautifully together in this charming room.

A SANTA MONICA FARMHOUSE

Moving from England to California half my life ago didn't seem as dramatic as it turned out to be. Santa Monica has been my American home ever since, and a wonderful place to bring up three active boys. During the twenty years of living on a palm-lined street embraced by mountain views, my Spanish Colonial Revival farmhouse has had many lives. It has seen bouncing castles in the front garden and petting zoos in the backyard; boogie boards, surfboards, skateboards and bikes on the driveway and around the pool deck; and trampled landscaping everywhere. The day finally arrived when I had the grounds all to myself, and I went to town. Even though the lot is somewhat tight, I didn't let that stop me from evoking the exotic gardens of a Moroccan courtyard with a Moorish fountain, colorful tile and bold displays of plant material. Apart from burnishing curb appeal, my front yard does double duty as overflow entertaining space and sets the tone for the rest of the house. And it provides a sense of privacy and enclosure once you're inside.

A *Parrot* painting by Hunt Slonem holds center court in the living room. Although an idiosyncratic blend of antique furniture and eccentric objects figure prominently here, the room still maintains a sense of uncluttered space. The Art Nouveau tile inset on the fireplace was a gift from a client. Club fender from KMI Studio.

The far wall fireplace rises to the peak of a double-height vaulted ceiling and adds a touch of grandeur to an otherwise intimate living room. The room also combines every element I love for a home's more communal spaces—comfortable furniture arranged for conversation and entertaining, good lighting, a knockout piece of contemporary art, and objects that reflect the owner's personality. Most importantly, it doesn't look "done" to perfection.

Personal treasures are so important in creating a home. Whether they're inherited portraits, family snapshots, or your child's artwork, you should be surrounded by the things that tell the story of your life arranged in a beautiful way. The delicately ornate Sicilian mirror was my earliest purchase as a young bride and is one of my most cherished possessions. I saw it one day at Gep Durenberger Antiques in San Juan Capistrano and simply had to have it, even though my husband and I lived in a leased, no-frills beach shack with corrosive salt air and zero wall space. The mirror now hangs over an eighteenth-century Italian marquetry chest that belonged to my grandfather.

Above:
A series of Afghani rugs sewn together creates a stairway runner for the limestone steps. The wrought-iron railing was installed in the '70s when the second floor was added.

Facing:
These 19th-century French bergéres are upholstered in a custom-embroidered sultan's robe by Martyn-Lawrence Bullard. Kashmiri hand-painted table from Vaughan. Balinese coffee table from KMI Studio.

Left:
When I renovated my kitchen, I ripped out all of the cabinetry and replaced it with open shelving. Not only is it a great way to display colorful dinnerware; it's also working example of my motto, "If you see it, you'll use it." By opening up an archway shared with the dining room and installing pocket doors, the kitchen easily becomes part of the flow of ground-floor living spaces. The day I realized that California was my permanent home, I splurged on an Aga, which diminished some of my homesickness. Another prized English import is the Damien Hirst print from his *Spot* series.

153

In the master suite, Gitana, my Jack Russell, relaxes on
the bed. Recently redecorated, the room is liberally
drenched with fabric from my latest collection, "Summers
in France." The palette in soft roses and corals is perfect
for L.A.—a city where lawns are always green and
roses bloom in winter. Tester trim from Scalamandré.
French Provincial mirror from the Furniture Cave in
London. Portraits of the boys by Nigel Waymouth.

Facing:
The KMI Wilbury armchair and ottoman has become an indispensable standard in my decorating work. This one is upholstered in my own "Moroccan Stripe" and comfortably occupies the nook overlooking the front garden. Standing lamp from Judy Greenwood, UK.

Above:
"Quilt" wallpaper in Pink/Rose Metallic and "Sheer Confetti" window fabric in Desert Rose both from Kathryn M. Ireland. Freestanding tubs are like having a piece of sculpture in the bathroom. I painted my vintage cast-iron claw-foot tub a bright pink enamel, "Hot Lips" by Benjamin Moore. Painting by Lucilla Smith. Bath accessories from Waterworks.

"Kathryn has an uncanny ability
to elevate secondary spaces—
hallways, niches, corners—into
memorable vignettes." —MEL BORDEAUX

Facing:
The guesthouse is an array of color from my "Mexico Meets Morocco" line, admittedly an untraditional and complex palette, but to me it's aromatherapy for the eyes. Barley twist bed and balustrade lamp in cast iron both from KMI Studio. Eighteenth-century Spanish side table from Hacienda, Ojai. Decorative objects locally sourced at the Santa Monica flea market, held on the first and fourth Sunday of every month at the Santa Monica Airport.

Above:
French doors open onto the pool area. As my real getaway house is in Europe, I simply convert my Santa Monica guesthouse into a weekend retreat. It's a refuge for creativity or relaxation or an exiled houseguest. Kathryn M. Ireland fabric and wallpaper. Antique Kashmiri lamp and shade from KMI online. Desk from KMI Studio furniture line.

A FRENCH BEACH HOUSE

One day I received a call from a couple in Texas on the hunt for a local French designer to help refresh a holiday home in Normandy, but it just wasn't in their DNA to hire a designer from the States for a job site in France. After scouring the region, the lady of the house—with magazine in hand—had convinced her husband that even though I was L.A.–based, my own summer home in France had just the right balance of authentic French country charm and North American conveniences they were looking for.

This turn-of-the-twentieth-century beach house had been handed down by French/English relatives for generations; my new clients were adamant that I preserve the atmosphere of a handsome, almost refined, rusticity. But the house was desperately short on bathrooms and had a woefully inept kitchen. I suggested we convert an attic space into a master bathroom, and, with a few other realistic goals, we created the updated home that my clients envisioned.

Above and right:
In this well-seasoned living
room, the beauty of the existing
paneling is enhanced by natural
light spilling in from tall windows
that frame ocean views. By
reupholstering existing pieces,
adding a comfortable deep
sofa, and filling in with antiques
sourced throughout France, we
pulled the room together without
it having a "redecorated" look.

Facing:
The kitchen was gutted and reorganized, rendering it clean and functional. A farmhouse table, provincial pottery and oversized terra-cotta tiles are not only practical for the beach; they also adhere to the local aesthetic, keeping the look traditional.

Above:
Installing glass French doors from the hallway into the kitchen made a big difference. It extended available sunlight further into the house.

Above:
A classic French bedside table original to the house is in the master bedroom. A new headboard was commissioned and the existing armchair was slip-covered.

Right:
The Kathryn M. Ireland blue floral "Ikat" is the lead fabric in the master. The clients' red embroidered chair adds the perfect touch of color.

Facing:
The new master bathroom was created in dead attic space. As a first step, we installed beadboard around the bathroom walls. Opening up the ceiling and adding a Victorian style bathtub allowed for necessary space and provided considerable charm.

Above:
Finding a vintage freestanding sink to complement the bath was a top priority for this room. Behind the curtain, simple shelving provides storage in an awkward space that would otherwise be unusable.

With lovely proportions, this room only needed a breath of fresh air to give it a lift. By reupholstering an existing chair and hanging floor-to-ceiling curtains on simple wooden rings, I maintained the turn-of-the-19th-century country feel that I was enlisted to preserve. Chair fabric is Kathryn M. Ireland "George" in khaki. Curtain fabric is Kathryn M. Ireland red "Boucle."

The easy, unpretentious note we hit is just right for a casual family summer home at the beach.

A BRENTWOOD ESTATE

When I turned my Santa Monica film editing room (from another life) into a shop for classic English decorative accessories, my relationship with the Newbergs began. Nancy, a talented jewelry designer and mother of three boys, was a frequent patron there. Years later, she hired me to help with her new home, designed by master architect Harry Newman.

Nancy and her husband, Bruce, are very artistic people and definitive in their tastes. Fortunately, Nancy and I work well as a team and can literally finish each other's sentences in regard to what we like and don't like. And when you have a client with distinctive style, her personality will always come through in the final result. The Newbergs' home, a vision of balance, texture, and subtle color, is clearly an expression of Nancy's smooth and artful sophistication.

The entry hall is filled with natural light. A romantic sweep of staircase is the centerpiece and underscores the sculptural quality of Newman's architecture.

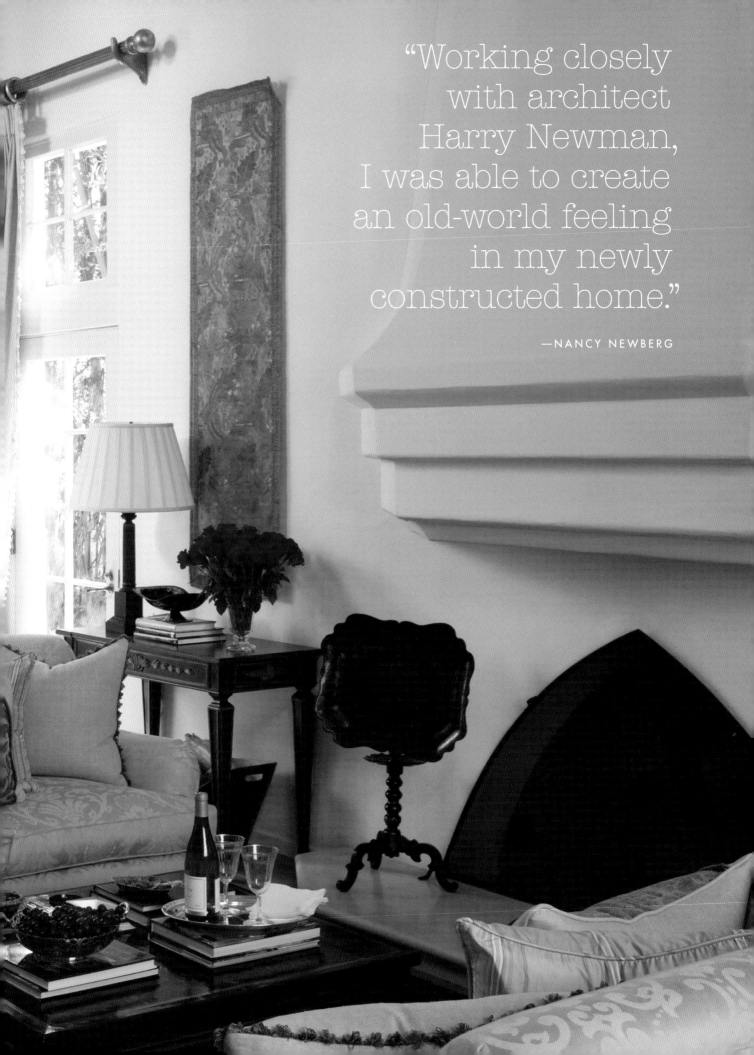

"Working closely
with architect
Harry Newman,
I was able to create
an old-world feeling
in my newly
constructed home."

—NANCY NEWBERG

Right:
All great dining rooms should
have romance; here it's
provided by the lofty ceiling
height, warm-hued plaster
walls, striking chandelier and
a grand window curtained
with hand-printed felt fabric
that Nancy found from a
dealer in London. Slip covers
on the chairs by Claremont.
Chinese sideboard from Lief,
West Hollywood. Lamps
from Lucca Antiques, West
Hollywood. Antique floor-
standing candleholders
found on 1stdibs. Chandelier
original to the home.

With arched windows, potted greenery and a moss color scheme, the kitchen conveys the impression of a conservatory on a grand estate. Nancy's collection of antique European pottery animates the wall space; the eggshell walls sans upper cabinets contribute to the sense of openness. The multifunctional oversized island is my dream. You can never have too much counter space!

"My East Coast roots dictated the importance of an elegantly aged yet timeless family home. Thick, hand-plastered walls with subtle architectural details such as curves, beams and arches throughout gave the house the charm I was after." —NANCY NEWBERG

Facing:
The soft color palette Nancy wanted throughout the house is beautifully expressed in an ethereal and calm bedroom. The reproduction English 19th-century four-poster canopy bed and coordinating bedside table are custom made by KMI Studio.

Nancy's affection for pale greens extends to the master bedroom suite. Two Fortuny fabrics, "Sevres" and "Alberelli," work gorgeously together in the sitting area and play off the creamy walls. Wilbury armchair and ottoman by KMI Studio. Nineteenth-century Chinese hand-painted armoire from Lief, West Hollywood.

Facing and above:

When you have an active family of boys, the pool
house becomes a heavily trafficked space. From
personal experience, I know that Mexican terra-
cotta pavers hold up well against endless to-ing
and fro-ing of wet feet. Vintage wicker coffee
table from Rooms & Gardens, Santa Monica. Throw
pillows from Calypso Home. Window treatment
fabric "Greta Indigo" and sofa fabric "Scroll Indigo"
from the Sanibel Collection by Kathryn M. Ireland.

A MALIBU BEACH HOUSE

One of the best aspects of my profession is the clients themselves—a cast of characters that have entered my life over the years as professional acquaintances and stayed on as great friends. Traci and Lucas Donat are no exception. Somewhat irrationally, my criterion for whom to work with is based on whether I would want to have them stay in my home in France! The Donats and their daughter, Lily, have become particularly beloved guests there. It was an immediate love fest among us from our first meeting. Like me, the Donats share a passion for the outdoors, growing their own vegetables and raising chickens. We understand the good life!

When Architect Douglas W. Burdge executed his unpretentious design of their new house in Malibu on the footprint of the old, he abandoned most of the original floor plan and architectural elements but added enough square footage to give the Donats all the room they needed for a relaxing home at the beach.

THE ENGLISH ROSES

Stirling Macoboy — The Ultimate Rose Book

FROM ALICE TO OCEAN

"This quintessential beach-style home was small in plan but big on space, as tall bifolding doors in the living areas create the ultimate indoor-outdoor relationship." —DOUGLAS W. BURDGE, AIA

"Kathryn's design aesthetic is unfussy.
Eclectic. A generous celebration of
life. She created an intimate home
that works whether you're coming
in from pushing a wheelbarrow,
entertaining, or returning from a
day at the beach." —LUCAS DONAT

The banquette, bookshelf, and desk area in Traci's office were built by Doug; my job was to accessorize with crisp blue and white fabrics. For the pillows, I used one-of-a-kind antique Balinese ikats I had found on a trip to Indonesia some years ago. C & C Milano ticking on the tufted mattress in marine blue and white keeps the space beachy.

Above:
The Kathryn M. Ireland "Moroccan" fabric for the curtains and Roman shade provides a sandy neutral backdrop for the splash of color in the rest of the room. Inlaid Syrian side tables from KMI Studio. Upholstered stools from Nathan Turner.

Facing:
Vintage mid-century metal lawn chairs from Hollywood at Home, West Hollywood. These beauties might have been designed for the outdoors, but the actual outdoors is practically an extension of this room and functions as an un-roofed den.

ACKNOWLEDGMENTS

Thank you, first of all, to all my friends and clients who so generously allowed me to photograph their homes: Leslie Burke, Joe and Debbie Mannis, David and Rebecca Mamet, Bill Guthy and Victoria Jackson, Bruce and Nancy Newberg, Robert and Leslie Zemeckis, David Heaney and Ann Lents, Lucas Donat and Traci Wald Donat.

Thank you to all the amazing architects that I got to work with on these projects—Andy Neumann, Marc Appleton, Cindy Grant, and Doug Burge—and to the landscape designers—Art Luna and Steven Block.

Thank you, Lucilla Smith and Ursula Brooks, for your eye for detail and for helping with photography.

Thank you, Mel Bordeaux, for overseeing and making corrections where necessary for the text.

Thank you, Tim Beddow, for all of the photography. Thanks also to Andreas Von Einsiedel for images of my home, to Victoria Pearson for the cover photograph and Ray Katchatorian for the back cover photograph.

Thank you to my construction and installation teams, in particular Kitchell, Nu-Vision Painting, Elite Transfer, Robert Ireland, Brian Ferrick, and Jan Scott. And a special thanks to Carl Perkins.

Thank you to Rita Sowins for the design, and to the Gibbs Smith team, in particular Madge Baird and Melissa Dymock.

RESOURCES

Amadi Carpets Inc.
408 N. Robertson Blvd.
West Hollywood, CA 90048
310.649.5353 Tel
310.652.0171 Fax
amadicarpets.com

Andy Neumann
Neumann Mendro Andrulaitis
Architects
888 Linden Ave.
Carpinteria,CA 93013
nmaarchitects.com

Ashbury Hides
1232 S. La Cienega Blvd., Ste. 104
Los Angeles, CA 90035
310.360.1520 Tel
310.360.1519 Fax
ashburyhides.com

Blanchard Antiques, London
Core One, the Gasworks
2 Michael Rd.
London SW6 2AN, UK
07863.729.487 Tel
jwblanchard.com

California Auctioneers
8597 N. Ventura Ave.
Ojai, CA 93001
805.649.2686 Tel
californiaauctioneers.com

Calypso St. Barth
calypsostbarth.com

Chelsea Editions New York
232 E. 59th St.
New York, NY 10022
212.758.0005 Tel
212.785.0006 Fax
chelseaeditions.com

de Le Cuona
D&D Building,
979 Third Ave., Ste. 914
New York, NY 10022
Contact: Susie Paplow
212.702.0800 Tel
212.702.9500 Fax
delecuona.co.uk

Dos Gallos Furniture
924 N. Formosa Ave.
Los Angeles, CA 90046
323.851.9117 Tel
dosgallos.com

Doug Burdge
Burdge & Associates
21235 Pacific Coast Hwy.
Malibu, CA 90365
buaia.com

Eccola
7408 Beverly Blvd.
Los Angeles, CA 90036
323.932.9922 Tel
323.932.9921 Fax
eccolaimports.com

Fortuny Inc.
979 Third Ave., Ste. 1632
New York, NY 10022
212.753.7153 Tel
212.935.7487 Fax
fortuny.com

Galerie Half
6911 Melrose Ave.
Los Angeles, CA 90038
323.424.3866 Tel
galeriehalf.com

Harry Newman, AIA
634 Tree Top Ln.
Thousand Oaks, CA 91360
harry91361@gmail.com

Henry Beguelin
8575 Melrose Ave.
West Hollywood, CA 90069
310.659.9320 Tel
310.358.9304 Fax
henrybeguelinusa.com

Hollyhock
927 N. La Cienega Blvd
Los Angeles, CA 90069
310.777.0100 Tel
310.777.0110 Fax
hollyhockinc.com

Hollywood at Home
724 & 750 N. La Cienega Blvd.
Los Angeles, CA 90069
310.273.6200 Tel
320.273.1438 Fax
hollywoodathome.com

Howe
93 Pimlico Road
London SW1W 8PH, UK
www.howelondon.com

Hunt Slonem
Marlborough Gallery
545 W. 25th St., 2nd Fl.
New York, NY 10001
marlboroughgallery.com

Indigo Seas
123 N Robertson Blvd
Los Angeles, CA 90048
310.550.8758 Tel

JF Chen
941 N. Highland Ave.
Los Angeles, CA 90038
310.559.2436 Tel
310.559.2437 Fax
jfchen.com

J. H. Minassian & Co.
Pacific Design Center
8687 Melrose Ave., Suite B139
Los Angeles, CA 90069
310.657.7000 Tel
310.657.6519 Fax
jhminassian.com

John Robshaw Textiles
245 W. 29th St., Ste. 1501
New York, NY 10001
212.594.6006 Tel
212.594.6116 Fax
johnrobshaw.com

Kathryn M. Ireland
Textiles & Design
636 N. Almont Dr.
West Hollywood, CA 90069
310.246.1906 Tel
kathrynireland.com

LA Home Boutique
Brentwood Country Mart
225 26th St., Unit 39
Santa Monica, CA 90402
310.587.0703 Tel

Lief Almont
646 N. Almont Drive
Los Angeles, CA 90069
310.492.0033 Tel
310.492.0026 Fax
liefalmont.com

Lucca Antiques
744 N. La Cienega Blvd.
Los Angeles, CA 90069
310.657.7800 Tel
310.657.7804 Fax
luccaantiques.com

Manuel Canovas
19–23 Grosvenor Hill
London, W1K 3QD, UK
44.020.8874.6484 Tel. Export Sales
44.020.8877.6420 Fax Export Sales
manuelcanovas.com

Mark Ransom
62–64 Pimlico Road
London SW1
www.markransom.co.uk

McKinney & Co.
Studio P, The Old Imperial Laundry
71 Warriner Gardens
London SW11 4XW, UK
44.0.20.7627.5077 Tel
mckinney.co.uk

Mosaic House
32 W. 22nd St.
New York, NY 10010
212.414.2525 Tel
212.414.2526 Fax
mosaichse.com

Nathan Turner
8546 Melrose Ave.
Los Angeles, CA 90069
310.275.1209 Tel
nathanturner.com

Obsolete
222 Main St.
Venice, CA 90291
310.399.0024 Tel
310.399.2155 Fax
obsoleteinc.com

Olivia Raeburn Decorative Painting
Los Feliz Blvd.
Los Angeles, CA 90027
213.618.8180 Tel
oliviaraeburn@sbcglobal.net

Pat McGann Gallery
246 N. La Cienega Blvd.
Los Angeles, CA 90069
310.657.8708 Tel
310.358.0977 Fax
patmcganngallery.com

Robert Kime
London Showroom:
121 Kensington Church St.
London W8 7LP, UK
44.020.7229.0886 Tel
44.020.7229.0766 Fax
robertkime.com
U.S. Agent:
John Rosselli & Associates
979 Third Ave., Ste. 1800
New York, NY 10022
212.593.2060 Tel
212.832.3687 Fax
johnrosselliassociates.com

Raoul Textiles
Pacific Design Center
8687 Melrose Ave., Ste. G-160
West Hollywood, CA 90069
310.657.4931 Tel
310.657.4934 Fax
raoultextiles.com

Rogers & Goffigon Ltd.
NY Showroom
979 3rd Ave., Ste. 1718
New York, NY 10022
212.888.3242 Tel

Rooms & Gardens
1311 Montana Ave., Ste. A
Santa Monica, CA 90403
310.451.5154 Tel
roomsandgardens.com

Ruby Beets
25 Washington St.
P.O. Box 1174
Sag Harbor, NY 11963
631.899.3275 Tel
rubybeets.com

Scalamandre
NY Office:
50 Wireless Blvd
Hauppauge, NY 11788
LA Showroom:
800–802 N. La Cienega Blvd
Los Angeles, CA 90069
310.657.8154 Tel

Shabby Chic
Montana Ave.
Santa Monica CA 90402
shabbychic.com

Stark Carpet
D&D Building
979 Third Ave., 11th Fl.
New York, NY 10022
212.752.9000 Tel
212.829.0352 Fax
starkcarpet.com

Vaughan Designs Inc.
D&D Building
979 Third Ave., Ste. 1511
New York, NY 10022
212.319.7070 Tel
212 319 7766 Fax
vaughandesigns.com

Waterworks
8580 Melrose Ave.
West Hollywood, Los
Angeles, CA 90069
310.289.5211 Tel
310.289.1028 Tel
waterworks.com

KMI SHOWROOMS

Charles Spada Interiors
Antiques on 5
1 Design Center Place, Ste. 232
Boston, MA 02210
charlesspada.com

Grizzel & Mann
Atlanta Decorative Arts Center
351 Peachtree Hills Ave., Ste. 120
Atlanta, GA 30305
404.261.5932 Tel
grizzelandmann.com

ID Collection
1025 Stemmons Freeway, Suite 745
Dallas, TX 75207
214.698.0226 Tel

John Brooks – Denver
2712 S. Broadway, Ste. L
Denver, CO 80209
303.698.9977 Tel
johnbrooksinc.com

John Brooks – Scottsdale
2712 N. 68th St.
Scottsdale, AZ 85257
480.675.8828 Tel

John Rosselli &
Associates – Chicago
222 Merchandise Mart Plaza, 6–158
Chicago, IL 60654
312.822.0760 Tel

John Rosselli &
Associates – Florida
Design Center of the Americas
1855 Griffin Rd., Ste. A-128
Dania, FL 33004
954.920.1700 Tel
johnrosselliassociates.com

John Rosselli & Associates
– New York
D&D Building
979 Third Ave., Ste. 701
New York, NY 10022
212.593.2060 Tel

John Rosselli & Associates – DC
1515 Wisconsin Ave., NW
Washington DC, 20007
202.337.7676 Tel

Scalamandre – Costa Mesa
2915 Red Hill Ave., Ste. B 106–107
Costa Mesa, CA 92626
713.627.8315 Tel
scalamandre.com

Scalamandre – Houston,
7026 Old Katy Rd., Ste. 103
Houston, TX 77055

Tissus d'Helene Ltd.
Chelsea Harbour Design Centre
421 The Chambers,
London SW10 0XF, UK
44.020.7352.9977 Tel